Every pastor is an interim pastor. Our role is to shepherd God's people until He calls us home or to a new ministry assignment. Many resources are available on beginning a ministry assignment; however, few have been written on how to transition out of one. Writing from experience, Bryant Wright shares the steps he and his leadership team took for a seamless passing of the baton to the next pastor. Succession is more than a manual for transition. It's a game plan for advancing the kingdom of God long after you're gone.

Robby Gallaty, pastor, Long Hollow Church
and author of *Recovered* and *Replicate*

Bryant writes with the vision of a senior Christian statesman and the wisdom of a long-time, faithful shepherd of God's people. Bryant is one of the most effective and Christ-like leaders I've ever known, and a lifetime of experience shines forth from this book. This book offers an up-close and personal look at how Bryant and his team handled this difficult process with grace and skill.

J.D. Greear, pastor at The Summit Church

Succession tells the detailed story of a transition that ultimately comes to all leaders. You will glean valuable truth and perspective from Bryant Wright as he shares how to do it right.

Johnny M. Hunt, senior VP of Evangelism
and Leadership at North American Mission
Board, pastor Emeritus at First Baptist
Woodstock, and former SBC president

Succession in the Bible brings comfort as we realize the ministry will continue and be strengthened. From Moses to Joshua and Paul to Timothy the biblical leadership baton is passed. Unfortunately, in today's ministry world the likelihood of concern outweighs comfort. It doesn't have to be that way. Let Bryant take you on an important and well-done journey of *Succession*.

Gregg Matte, pastor of Houston's First Baptist Church and author of *Capture the Moment* devotional

Bryant Wright is one of those rare individuals who always seems to just get it right and do it right. He pulled off one of the most difficult feats for a leader, which is a successful succession process. Leaders from every walk of life should get this book and devour it! They will be glad they did, and I say that right from my heart!

James Merritt, senior pastor at Cross Pointe Church

Succession is a must read for any church leadership facing the challenge of moving from one pastor to the next. It is an enjoyable, easy read, filled with great wisdom and insight. Any church's pastoral succession will be far more successful by having its leadership read this book.

Randy Pope, founding pastor of Perimeter Church and president of Life on Life Ministries

It has been a privilege to witness the wisdom and practical insight of this book as I watched my dad prayerfully approach succession with the desire to finish strong and prepare the church for even greater days after his pastoral leadership had come to an end. Johnson Ferry stands out as a beautiful example of succession done right! As a pastor who has experienced succession on the receiving side of this conversation, I highly recommend this book to those who are seeking to finish strong and those who are seeking to build on the legacy they have received.

George Wright, senior pastor at Shades Mountain Baptist Church

SUCCESSION

SUCCESSION

Preparing Your

MINISTRY

for the Next

LEADER

Bryant Wright

BRYANT WRIGHT

with **CLAY SMITH**

B&H
PUBLISHING
NASHVILLE, TENNESSEE

This book is dedicated to the wonderful people of Johnson Ferry Baptist Church who supported this succession process. Their support for our succession process was one of the many great blessings of being their pastor.

ACKNOWLEDGMENTS

Beginning with Executive Assistants Olivia Mahon, Ashley Ammons, and Kelly Lamb. Without their dedicated assistance, this book would never have come to fruition.

To William Vanderbloemen and Tim Stevens, our consultant, with Vanderbloemen Search Group.

To the editorial staff and team at Lifeway who have been very helpful in every step along the way.

To Randy Pope, a long-time prayer partner for more than thirty years.

To Clay Smith, God's chosen man to be my successor.

To the Johnson Ferry Baptist Church Pastor Search Team, who were all uniquely called to lead in the succession process.

To the members and attenders of Johnson Ferry Baptist Church, who experienced the whole process of succession unfold right before their eyes.

And, as always, to my wife, Anne, who shares in ministry with me and offers valuable input and reflection about the core message of this book. We went through the process of succession as one.

CONTENTS

FOREWORD

Little did I know that a voicemail would change my life. I was sitting across a lunch table with a good friend when my phone started to buzz. Thus, the awkward moment. Do you give in to your inner FOMO and look at the screen or do you be fully present with the person in front of you? I sheepishly chose the former. The name *Bryant Wright* illuminated in my hand. I pushed it to voicemail and finished the lunch. An hour later I sat in my car and listened to the message. *Hey Clay, this is Bryant Wright, I'd love to visit with you over the phone at your convenience.* I called Bryant back, engaged in a little small talk and then he made a life-altering statement. *Clay,* he said, *I want to ask you to pray about putting your name forward as a candidate to be my successor at*

Johnson Ferry. I do not remember what I said next but it was probably some ministerial affirmation that I'd certainly pray about it. I started the car, drove back to the church I pastored and moved on with the day.

I first met Bryant Wright when I was a college student at the University of South Carolina. His son was a friend and we ate with Bryant and Anne a few times as they would travel to town. I knew he was a pastor and that the church he led was in Atlanta. That was about it. Fast forward seventeen years, Bryant had reached out to me to be a part of a young pastor mentor group. I, along with five other young pastors, was asked to meet quarterly for two years to learn from Bryant and the ministry of Johnson Ferry. I initially declined to be a part due to scheduling conflicts throughout the year. But Bryant let me know of a second group made up of large church pastors who had recently succeeded long-tenured ministries. Though I did not fit that exact profile, he invited me to join. I agreed and found a fast friendship with this group, though our current ministry roles were very different. They were all traversing the treacherous road of pastoral succession, helping large healthy churches adjust to a new leader for a new generation. This group proved to be both helpful and providential in the plans God would unfold for my life.

In hindsight, it would seem like the choice to be considered for a church like Johnson Ferry was an easy *yes*. But it wasn't. I loved the church I was pastoring. It was a legacy church and we had seen God do much in the way of health, revitalization, and growth. I was nearing five years there with plans for a decade more. *But that phone call.* A mentor of mine told me to always pray about the ministry opportunities that I did not seek out. These have a way of either confirming your love for the place you serve or opening you up to a new assignment from God. My wife, Terrica and I began praying about it and felt led to being considered a candidate. Psalm 143:8–10 (NIV) became a central passage for us:

> Let the morning bring me word of your
>   unfailing love,
>   for I have put my trust in you.
> Show me the way I should go,
>   for to you I entrust my life.

> Rescue me from my enemies, Lord,
>> for I hide myself in you.
> Teach me to do your will,
>> for you are my God;
> may your good Spirit
>> lead me on level ground.

Four months later, after countless prayers, phone calls, video conferences, lunches, and trips to Atlanta, we and the pastor search team came to the mutual conclusion that I would be the next pastor to lead the ministry of Johnson Ferry. We said our long and tearful goodbyes to people we dearly loved in Charlotte and began the transition to living in Atlanta.

Most of what I was feeling was a mixture of excitement and dread. The excitement stemmed from the opportunities presented for ministry at Johnson Ferry, plus the fact that we sensed God's clear call to come. But there was also dread. I had heard horror stories of pastoral transitions. *What if I cannot do this? What if I am not a fit here? What if they don't follow through on their promises? What if their greatest days are behind them? You never want to follow a founder, right? You want to be the guy after the guy.* These were the unhealthy scripts sneaking into my heart.

Gratefully, none of them came true. God has done a great work to bring about a healthy transition from one leader to another. And what you will read in this book will tell you why. God gets the credit, but He used a lot of good people to do it. Bryant exhibited both humility and intentionality without which this transition would not have been possible. The elders used wisdom and foresight to craft an effective strategy. And the people of Johnson Ferry have been nothing but supportive and encouraging to the pastor God has called to lead them. It is truly a God story and this book will help you know the way that He can do the same with your church.

I believe Johnson Ferry's best days are in her future. And I pray the same is true for your church as you pass the leadership baton to the next generation.

Clay Smith
Senior Pastor, Johnson Ferry Baptist Church

INTRODUCTION

It was the summer of 2012. My wife and I were enjoying a much-needed sabbatical after two demanding years of having two full-time jobs— pastoring a megachurch and serving as president of the Southern Baptist Convention. I had recently read Bob Russell's book, *Transition Plan*, where he writes about the succession plan he led at Southeast Christian Church where he had pastored for forty years.

It led me to think seriously about the future. I was sixty years old, the founding pastor of Johnson Ferry Baptist Church. I did not feel a pastor could be more blessed by such a supportive congregation. Johnson Ferry had embraced the mission of Jesus in being a Great Commission congregation. There was nothing on earth I would rather do than pastor Johnson Ferry. I also had no interest in ever retiring. But I was sixty years old. No pastor lives forever. Pastoring Johnson Ferry had been the greatest thirty years of my life. But at the end of the day, all pastors are really "interim pastors"—entrusted by God to shepherd His people for a season. The next ten years would fly by, and we needed to make some plans. So, when the sabbatical was over, I was convicted by the Lord that I needed to get with the elders of the church and develop a succession plan.

This is my story. This is our church's story. This became our succession story. I hope it helps pastors, churches, and any leaders of ministries and organizations who grapple with the challenge of succession.

Chapter 1

MEETING WITH THE ELDERS IN 2013

While on sabbatical in the summer of 2012, I read Bob Russell's great book, *Transition Plan*. The premise of the book revolves around the process of a pastor approaching the elders about a succession plan. He wrote that when the elders approach the pastor about a succession plan, it is a firing plan. But when the pastor approaches the elders about a succession plan, it is truly a succession plan. I had been the pastor at Johnson Ferry Baptist Church (JFBC) for thirty years in 2012. The milestone of taking on my fourth decade in ministry got my attention. As one of Ten Big Goals that God had put on my heart for the fourth decade at JFBC, I set the goal of developing a succession plan with the church elders. We began this discussion in 2013.

Surprise

Initially, they were surprised. I was only sixty years old. The church was doing well. I was the only pastor the church had ever had, and every staff member had come to Johnson Ferry under my leadership. Just bringing up the topic caught them by surprise. In many ways it was a surprise to me as well. A part of me still saw myself as the young pastor planting a new church in the north Atlanta suburbs. Obviously those days were over.

Appreciation

It's a reality in life that when a long-tenured pastor turns sixty, people begin to wonder, *How much longer is he going to be here?* Before my 2012 sabbatical, some people started to ask me those types of questions. "When are you going to hang it up?" "How much longer you going to stay with it?" "Now that you have been the president of the Southern Baptist Convention, what's next for you?" Those were new questions in my tenure. The elders were even beginning to get them from church members as well. So they were thankful that I brought it to the table.

Relief

They were relieved that this would not be immediate. I had no plan to retire any time soon. In fact, I told them I would love to keep at it until about seventy. That would give me a little more than forty years as their pastor. The number also seemed to be biblically appropriate—forty is big in the Bible.

The Study

As we began discussing the matter, one of the first decisions we made was to read Bob Russell's book and discuss what we learned. It would be different for us. Bob's successor, Dave Stone, was on their staff for many years before it was publicly announced that he would be taking on Bob's role. And even then, it would be many years before Dave would actually become their senior pastor. We did not envision an overlap transition time to last that long.

That thought was reinforced as I began to have interviews with retired pastors who had positive succession experiences. I also did this with some of their successors to gain their perspective on the process. It was unanimous among the successors that six months was plenty of time for a transition. This came from successors who had experienced a transition time of six months or longer. The message was clear. If the successor is a leader and feels called to lead, he is not going to want to wait too long. Dave Stone is a real exception of a fine leader who could follow the long-term plan that he and Bob did at Southeast Christian Church.

It was also helpful that I asked Dave to speak at Johnson Ferry as we were going through this study. He was even gracious enough to include a meeting with our elders when I scheduled him to speak at our leadership banquet. We enjoyed having his perspective in person. It is difficult to argue with success, and Southeast Christian was greatly blessed in their transition from Bob to Dave. His insight was beyond helpful.

Long-Tenured Pastor's Advice

The long-tenured pastors who had retired also had valuable insight that I shared with the elders.

1. Administrative Assistant

Be sure they provide you at least a part-time administrative assistant. Ministry does not stop with retirement from the pastorate. Correspondence, speaking invitations, travel plans, appointments, etc. continue to come.

2. Office Space

The counsel was varied about whether office space should be at the church or at another location, but the consensus leaned toward having an office at another location so that the new pastor wouldn't feel that I had never left. But if the office was to be off campus, asking the elders to provide funds for the office rental would be a great help.

3. Ministry Funds

Expenses will continue. Not everyone pays all the expenses for speaking engagements or mission trips. Funds are needed for lunch appointments, books and periodicals, travel for denominational meetings or seminars. This could be everything from the annual SBC convention or just a meeting I would be asked to attend as a former president of the SBC.

The elders agreed to plan for all these suggestions. It sure helps to have supportive, big-thinking elders serving with you.

Chapter 2

"MAKING A PLAN"

By 2014, the seven elders (five laymen, the deacon chairman, and the senior pastor) settled on a plan we would present to the church later that year. It was a threefold plan.

Scenario 1: Catastrophic Plan

This would be the plan if I died suddenly. (I called it the "Sudden Death" plan, but one of our elders felt "catastrophic" sounded better.) It would also cover the possibility of my becoming incapacitated or falling into moral failure. In this plan, where the church unexpectantly or suddenly found itself with no pastor, we addressed several plans of action:

1. I would collect names of outstanding young pastors I knew personally or by reputation and update it annually with a file folder in my executive assistant's desk. With this list, the elders or a pastor's search committee would have a place to start.

2. I would leave a confidential folder in my executive assistant's desk of the executive pastor on our staff I felt was best suited to begin to serve in the role of interim staff leader. We agreed to keep this confidential, for we had four men in addition to myself on the executive staff team. At the time, they were all long-tenured staff and outstanding in their roles in leading their portion of the church staff on a day-to-day basis. I didn't want any of them to feel resentful if I recommended one of them over the other in these years of preparation. It would be easier on their relationships with one another for me to keep it confidential (and of course easier on me knowing that if and when they found out I would be in heaven enjoying life and would avoid the possible hurt feelings from the three who were not designated as "the guy").

3. Each year I would give an update to the elders at our annual elders retreat in January. This was good accountability for me to continue to build the list of young pastors who might be a possible successor.

Scenario 2: A Potential Successor on the Staff

In this scenario, if we had an outstanding young minister on our staff who was gifted in preaching and leadership (two absolutely essential gifts for any megachurch pastor), then I would go to the elders and let them know I felt the time had come to recommend that minister as my successor. This, of course, would be the elders' decision. They might not feel he is God's man for the role. Still, we all agreed that if there was a possible successor on the staff, it would be overwhelmingly evident to us all when that time comes. For many years, I have called young men to be teaching pastors on our staff. They all have had a day-to-day ministry they are responsible for (young adults, college, etc.). But they all have a calling to preach and to eventually pastor a church of their own. The idea was for each of them to serve three to five years as a teaching pastor and then be sent out from Johnson Ferry to pastor somewhere else. It has been an investment in the kingdom. It began with one young man graduating from seminary. Then, over time, it grew from one to two teaching pastors who began to emerge among younger members of our staff. In the last five years of my tenure, we had three teaching pastors at once.

Increasingly through the years, I had teaching pastors preach more Sundays per year as I preached less. With five or six Sunday morning services during those years and two completely separate venues with two radically different styles of worship, they had plenty of opportunities to preach. By the time my succession plan was implemented in 2018, they were preaching from ten to twelve Sundays a year.

This frequency kept gradually increasing as I began to recognize a need for a break from preaching every six to eight weeks. On the weeks I wasn't preaching, I worked on long-term planning and sermon series. This also prepared the congregation by hearing different voices of young preachers in the pulpit. It was good for them and good for Johnson Ferry.

Scenario 3: A Search for a Successor Outside of Johnson Ferry

If I felt led to hand off the pastor role to a younger man outside of our staff, then I would go to the elders and share that I felt the time was right for us to begin a search process. Then I would bring a recommended search team to the elders for their approval and ultimately the church's approval. They would have the right to suggest other names that should be added or strike any names they did not feel should be in that role. With this scenario, that list of young pastors that I would be building and keep on file would be important for the search team to begin their process.

The Implementation of the Plan

1. Once we completed this process, the elders said to me, "Okay, Bryant, it's in your court. Let us know when the Lord lets you know it is time." That was affirming. I know many pastors would be

apprehensive about bringing up succession planning with their key church lay leaders. We all have fears: "If I bring it up, will they assume I'm ready to leave?" "Will they go ahead and suggest that I move on?" I had some of those fears myself. But as the plan became clear, I could sense how thankful the elders were that I initiated the process. After all, when a pastor is in his sixties, the church is naturally going to wonder, *How much longer will the pastor be here?* Still, lay leaders are often hesitant to raise the question themselves. They fear it could make the pastor think they want him to go. I realized that the elders were thinking, *This is one of the most important times of leadership for the future of the church that our pastor has ever led us to do.*

2. The elders felt it would be wise to inform the church in conference about the succession plan and then ask for their affirmation. At first I was uneasy. I preferred to keep it between me and the elders. If we did that, would the congregation begin to think I was about to retire? Would they view me as a lame duck? The elders, however, felt that the church would be relieved to know we had a plan. This would be done in one of our

semiannual conferences on a Wednesday night. The attendance at these conferences was normally low. We have hundreds and hundreds involved in a number of ministries as well at a fellowship meal on Wednesday nights during the school year. But in the room where the conference is, few come. When I say a small number, I mean small. We probably average fewer than one hundred in attendance twice a year. This is not a sign of apathy. It is a sign of trust in the leaders. I tell younger pastors who feel deflated when small crowds show up for church conferences, "The only time you have high attendance in a church conference is when there is a big problem in the church. Be thankful they trust your leadership."

The elders felt it would be important for one of them to tell the people at the conference that I had approached them over a year earlier feeling we needed a succession plan. This was important for those in attendance to know that I had initiated the process and not them. That elder would also make clear that "Bryant has no plan to retire any time soon. He hopes to be here another seven to eight years at least." Then, once the plan was affirmed by those in attendance, I would get up and reassure them that I had no plan to retire for many years. It would allow me to let those in attendance know how thankful I was that the elders had worked together to have a game plan in place.

Amazingly, after that small church conference, we had no fires to put out concerning rumors within the congregation that "Bryant is about to retire." The church knew I had been their founding pastor and had served for over thirty years. No one stays forever. The elephant in the room had been addressed. Those in attendance were thankful that the elders had a plan in place.

Chapter 3

THE CONSULTANT AND THE EXECUTIVE STAFF

As our process of annual updates on the succession plans continued, we brought in William Vanderbloemen, the founder of Vanderbloemen Search Group: a specialized search firm that focuses on assisting churches and ministries in finding new pastors and staff. We had read his book *Next*, written with Warren Bird, on pastoral succession. He spent time with the elders and our executive staff and a few key ministers on our staff in a one-day consultation. His insight and observations were helpful. He was also able to get a read on the culture of Johnson Ferry. This is crucial when the time comes for matching qualified candidates with a specific church or ministry.

Out of his one-day consultation with us, he returned with helpful suggestions for us to consider: (1) he affirmed the steps we had already taken, and (2) he helped us begin to think of other areas we had not yet considered. First, we had to realize how important the retiring senior pastor's wife is to this whole process. So often the problems in succession have to do with the retiring pastor's wife. She is hugely influential in the success or failure of the transition. She is letting go of a whole way of life she has lived for fifteen to twenty, sometimes thirty years or more. Most of her closest friends are in the church. What will she do in the future? What will be her role in the process? If she has questions about the new man or how he is leading in the future while she is still a member of the church, it can be disruptive within the church. So right away my wife Anne and I began to talk about this. She did not like thinking about that kind of pressure.

Second, William affirmed what the elders had planned for me in providing a part-time ministry assistant, office space, and ministerial expenses when I retire. But he said our elders needed to do more. He told the elders, "You need to give Bryant and Anne a fully paid sabbatical for a designated time when he finishes at Johnson Ferry. This will be a much-deserved rest for them, but most of all, it will allow the new pastor to become the pastor of the church. This needs to be announced to the church as a whole when Bryant leaves." William also suggested for us to give thought to a length of time to paying the pastor's salary or a portion of his salary after the sabbatical is completed in appreciation for his more than thirty years of service.

He explained that this is helpful to the retiring pastor to know exactly what he will face financially without wondering if he is going to be able to make it. He can plan more intelligently. The worst thing is for a pastor hanging on a few years longer than he should just to be financially secure. The elders agreed they would work on that.

Finally he pointed out that all four of our executive staff were also long-tenured (from twenty to thirty years together), and they were all baby boomers like me. He urged us to give thought to a smooth succession plan for each of them, knowing some of them might retire before I did. (Two of the four would do so.) These men all had great authority and the responsibility of leading a large portion of our staff. When it came time for them to retire, who followed them would be hugely important. One suggestion was for each executive staff person to begin to target and groom a successor to follow him. The person being groomed would not have to be told this because over time, for various reasons, it might not work out. Yet, in the meantime, the elders and I would know who that person would be. They could occasionally bring that person into executive staff and elders meetings to give reports to see them in action. All of this is just responsible preparation for the future.

Annual Reviews

Each year after that we had the executive staff come to a portion of our annual elders retreat and share an update of their ministry. It was especially helpful that the two who retired before me were comfortable sharing their plans with me more and more before their retirement. They knew the elders had a succession plan for me and they were thankful to know their roles were of great importance. They trusted the process we were prepared to implement.

Chapter 4

THE CONVERSATION

In the spring of 2016, three and a half years after this process began, I began to sense my time at Johnson Ferry might be coming to an end sooner than I expected. My son, who many in Johnson Ferry had assumed would become my successor because he had been pastoring a Johnson Ferry church plant successfully, was called to pastor a large church in South Carolina. It was the church he and his wife had been a part of in their college years and was where he served on staff before going to seminary. He followed a friend and peer of mine who was retiring after serving as pastor there for thirty-eight years. Anne and I were so excited for him. He was going to a great church. Additionally, we knew that he would have the opportunity to be out of his dad's shadow in the metro Atlanta area. But at the same time, we also realized that his becoming my successor would now be a real long shot. If I retired in the next two to three years, it would be unlikely that he would want to leave that great church so soon. It is a church that has been a major influence for Christ in that city.

As I watched that whole process of his calling to that church unfold, I found myself intrigued as to how the pastor and church leaders were shepherding the church through that transition. I realized that we could learn a great deal from them, and it began to be on my mind more and more. I wondered how I would know the time was right.

I kept thinking back to when I was in college and would ask people, "How do you know you have met the right girl to marry?" Time and again the answer people gave me was, "You'll just know." That answer always frustrated me. That was no help at all. But then I met my wife and I just knew. She was the one God was leading me to marry. Now, forty-seven years later, that still remains true.

I wondered, *Would that be how God would let me know it was time to let go of pastoring Johnson Ferry—a church my wife and I loved, the only church I have served as a full-time pastor and the only pastor they had ever had?*

Then, in the spring of 2017, I was walking to the parking lot with one of our elders after an elders meeting. We were discussing millennials—how they just look at things differently. He is in commercial construction and observes this all the time in buildings that appeal to them. He said, "Bryant, take our atrium for example." (It is a huge gathering place for the people at Johnson Ferry—a three-story open-air foyer that looks like a mall.) "A millennial walks into our atrium and immediately knows this is not a church for them." I asked, "What do you mean?" He replied, "They immediately know it is a church for boomers." Defensively, I replied, "I love our atrium. It's beautiful." He said, "Of course, you think that! You're a boomer! But it is too nice, too traditional. It's not a look they identify with."

I drove home and told my wife, "I think I'm toast." She looked up. "What? Was the meeting that bad? It couldn't have been that bad, could it? The church is so healthy."

I said, "No, the meeting was great. The spirit was good. It has nothing to do with the meeting."

She looked puzzled and asked, "What do you mean then?"

I told her about the conversation I had just had with the elder and how I realized while driving home that he was exactly right. I see it everywhere. When I go where millennials gather, whether in churches or office spaces, there is a definite look. Then I said to my wife, "I think I'm toast because I will never intuitively think like a millennial. I've been able to do it for thirty-five years with boomers and to a lesser degree with Gen Xers."

Millennials fascinate me. I'm constantly reading and studying how they think, but they have grown up in a completely different world. Still, I'll never be able to think like them, and I have no desire or interest in leading our church through another capital campaign to redesign and remodel our facility to connect with millennials. That's a job better suited for my successor.

That spring night, in the conversation with that elder that had nothing to do with succession, I just knew. The time was coming—sooner than I expected. I had some serious praying to do.

Chapter 5

CONVERSATIONS WITH ANNE

At the beginning of 2017, I discussed the succession plan more and more with my wife. She was not interested in thinking about it. We both love Johnson Ferry. I've often thought, *I don't see how a church could be more supportive of their pastor than Johnson Ferry is with us*. We never seriously considered another church. But knowing it is God's church and not ours, when other churches would contact me to see if I would be open to coming to be their pastor, I always tried to stay open to God's will and pray about what was put before me. Not one time did I feel any serious conviction from the Lord that He was calling us to another church.

But this was different. I was beginning to feel my days were coming to an end at Johnson Ferry. I had no desire to pastor anywhere else. There was just a "sameness" about pastoring Johnson Ferry that made me feel that I was moving into more of a "maintenance mode" than a "growth mode" as a pastor. That was something I desperately wanted to avoid.

It was also depressing me that we couldn't do anything to stop a slight annual decline in our worship attendance over the previous ten years. At this point attendance had dropped about 10 percent from our peak ten years earlier. Weekly Bible study attendance kept inching up. Budget giving was increasing dramatically (except for 2009–2010 during the economic recession), but we had more than recovered from that. We continued to average between 250 and 300 new members each year. More than five thousand adults (two-thirds of our adult members) were serving in some kind of ministry. And most exciting of all, we were now averaging about two thousand adults and teenagers going on seventy to eighty mission trips around the globe every single year. Aside from the worship attendance, the church was healthy. But what I kept thinking was, *I am the pastor—the preacher. I can't figure out how to reverse this trend in worship attendance.* I couldn't help but compare it to our first twenty to twenty-five years when the worship attendance growth was rising dramatically every single year.

Part of this was a cultural change in worship attendance. We knew people were attending less frequently. That was happening all over the country, but we were dealing with another significant trend. At Johnson Ferry, we had two styles of worship: traditional and contemporary. Each style had three worship services in two venues (for a total of six Sunday morning services). The attendance for traditional worship was falling while contemporary worship was rising. I felt like we were needing to go from three to two traditional worship services to simply have a critical mass of people in the room.

It wasn't just that. I kept telling my wife, "It may be time for a younger man who will intuitively think like millennials to reach the next generation." Anne, however, still didn't want to think about it. She loves Johnson Ferry and has so many meaningful relationships in our church. She began to say, "You just need a break—a vacation." I would reply, "I'm not tired!" But she didn't believe me.

The summer of 2017 came with my annual July vacation break. Yet during and after a great vacation, my feelings about the future hadn't changed. Then, as the year was winding down and those conversations continued, she began to say, "I just think you need a sabbatical—to completely let go and get your batteries fully charged again." But unlike other years in the church when I felt like I was running on fumes—trying to make it to the next sabbatical, I didn't feel any need for an extended break or time away. God had not made clear to her that it was time.

Chapter 6

VISION AND MISSION ARE NOT THE SAME

Before Christmas of 2017, I went to lunch with a longtime prayer partner, Randy Pope. We had been prayer partners for over twenty years. Both of us were founding pastors of churches that God had greatly blessed. His Perimeter Church had become one of the largest Presbyterian (PCA) churches in the U.S. Though our denominational traditions differ, founding pastors of megachurches have more in common with one another than with many churches in their own denominations.

We had continued discussions about succession that we had been having for a while. I told him I felt like it was coming for me sooner than I had planned. He then shared with me that he was getting close as well. He told me that at a recent gathering of pastors of the larger churches in the PCA, they heard John Piper speak about how he was led to retire. Piper said he "began to lack vision for his church's future." That was me completely.

It was another moment like that conversation I had had earlier that year with one of our elders. I realized that lacking vision for the future was exactly what I was dealing with and had been dealing with for the first time as a pastor.

Jesus clearly articulates the mission of the church. His Great Commission for the church is "to make disciples from all nations." The Greek word for *nations* is "ethnos" from which we get our words, *ethnic* and *ethnicity*. Missiologists call them "people groups."

Jesus knew that nations' names and geographical boundaries would constantly change over the years. But *ethnos* (people groups) stay generally the same in language and cultural distinctions. Missiologists tell us there are more than eleven thousand people groups on the planet. Of those, more than seven thousand are considered largely unreached with the gospel and of the seven thousand plus, about three thousand have no known

Christian, church, or ministry sharing the gospel. Obviously, the unchanging mission of the church still has a long way to go. But here is an exciting sideline. In 2011, the estimated number of unreached and unengaged people groups was not three thousand but more than thirty-eight hundred. This is the largest and fastest drop in the two thousand plus years of the church. The Holy Spirit is moving powerfully through so many evangelical ministries across the world to take the gospel to the most unreachable places. Some of these locations are isolated geographically, and many others are greatly restrictive because of totalitarian or Muslim regimes. These are exciting days for each church to join in what God is doing around the world.

For a Christ-centered congregation the mission is clear. Still, the vision for the local church is what God puts in the minds and hearts of pastors who lead individual churches. Usually, this vision is supported and enriched by other key leaders in the church, but the pastor is the main driver under the leadership of the Holy Spirit.

Vision includes specifics of *how* the church will carry out Christ's Great Commission. What will be the approach to ministry? What new ministries need to be added? Where do we need to give more or less emphasis? Will more facility or land space be needed? What new staff should be added? We can go on and on. The vision of the pastor is not the mission of the church. The mission never changes, but the vision of the pastor for the local church is constantly evolving through the leadership of the Holy Spirit.

Earlier I mentioned ten big goals for my fourth decade of ministry at Johnson Ferry from 2012–2021. Coming up with a succession plan with the elders was one of the ten. But what was bearing on my mind was by the end of 2017 (halfway through the fourth decade) was that God had already fulfilled nine out of ten. The only unfulfilled one was the purchase of a two-acre plot on land right beside the church where a widow was living. For more than twenty-five years, the church had hoped to purchase her land. But after all these years, even though the church's property now surrounded her on every side, she was still not interested in selling. That was obviously out of our control.

So, during 2017, I began praying regularly, "Lord, what new vision do You want me to have for Johnson Ferry in the second half of this fourth decade of ministry?" Silence. Then more silence. But amid that silence, there was a dominant focus on succession planning that went beyond coming up with a plan. That dominant focus, now the fresh vision, was implementing the plan sooner than I expected.

I had been hoping to go to seventy years old. It sounded good. Forty years of pastoring Johnson Ferry at seventy years old had nice round numbers, too. It was easy to comprehend those even numbered decades of life and ministry. It just made sense. God's timing, however, was not my timing.

As these thoughts intensified, I found myself pushing back with the Lord in other areas. Some were significant. Some were slightly embarrassing. The significant ones were: (1) How would this affect the staff? Beginning a church plant with a staff of one (me) meant every person on our staff had come under my leadership. I love these people and was especially grateful for the incredibly long tenure of so many of our ministerial staff. It would be unsettling for them to begin to serve under a brand-new young pastor. (2) I loved the weekly rhythm of pastoring. The study for the Sunday sermon, the preaching of the Sunday services, the rhythm of weekly ministry. What would it be like to let go of that? (3) The support of the lay leaders—the elders, the deacons, and a multitude of lay leaders in a seven-day-a-week church meant a lot to me. Anne and I were so thankful for these people and the many meaningful relationships built over thirty-six years of ministry.

The embarrassing concerns were: (1) I dreaded the thought of losing the platform of being pastor of Johnson Ferry, both in the denomination and in the community. I am realistic about how many relationships and opportunities for leadership would change and even diminish over time when I was no longer the pastor of the church. I didn't look forward to that reality. (2) Having adequate resources for retirement concerned me. The church had been so good to us in this area for so many years. We couldn't be more blessed. Still, the numbers our financial planner had been sharing with us in our retirement planning if I pastored Johnson Ferry until I was seventy were significant and enticing. I realize understanding our financial plan is good responsible stewardship of the Lord's resources that he has entrusted to us. But it made me sick to think about pastoring a few more years simply to have a better nest egg for retirement. That was not a noble reason for staying. It's embarrassing to confess that I was even arguing with myself that I would be better off hanging on three or four more years for financial reasons when God had always met our needs and always will.

Anne's Turning Point—Spring of 2018

With the question of whether the Lord was leading me to implement the plan for succession heavy on my mind, a key event helped Anne and me come to a greater acceptance that it was time. In the spring of 2018, I was contacted by a ministry that really intrigued me. They asked if I would be willing to lead it as their next CEO. It would involve a great challenge and allow me to focus on an area of ministry where I was passionate. They were just at the stage of contacting possible candidates. My name would just be one among many being contacted. I committed to pray about it and told them I would consider it. Over the next couple of months, I found myself thinking about it constantly. I wrote down dreams of how the ministry could be used in a great way for building up Christ's kingdom. As Anne and I had more conversations about it, she realized that my heart was more excited about this new possibility than pastoring Johnson Ferry.

Even though the door closed on that ministry possibility, Anne saw that I didn't need a break, a vacation, or a sabbatical. She began to sense that God was changing my heart away from pastoring Johnson Ferry. It certainly reinforced that for me.

Sabbatical—Summer of 2018

We were scheduled for a sabbatical in the summer of 2018. Both of us knew that God had put one primary focus on our hearts to pray about: Was the timing right to implement the plans for succession? I was pretty confident it was. Anne was now beginning to think so as well, but we both felt this sabbatical was coming at a perfect time to withdraw from Johnson Ferry Baptist Church for about ten weeks. During this time, we could not only pray for God's will to be crystal clear, but we also would have plenty of time to discuss other possibilities for ministry in the future. It could also help us look at how I felt being away from Johnson Ferry during that ten-week period. All our previous sabbaticals had been about rest, family time, reading, and learning about other ministries that could enrich Johnson Ferry. This one would be different.

I didn't feel tired and in need of rest. Our boys were all grown and had families of their own. Learning of other possible ministries in the local church held little interest. There was one thing on our minds: Was God leading us to hand off the role of pastoring Johnson Ferry to a younger man?

During that sabbatical, God clearly confirmed to us that the timing was right. Part of what the Lord did on that sabbatical that was different from others was how I felt about being away from the pulpit of Johnson Ferry. During every other sabbatical, I would begin to get antsy about preaching again by the fifth or sixth week. Sermon ideas would always begin to flood my yellow legal pads along with new ideas for pastoring Johnson Ferry. On this sabbatical, however, that did not occur. The yellow legal pad stayed basically empty except for one thing—a time frame for implementing and carrying out the plan for succession. That was combined with a perfect peace for doing so.

Yet, to be absolutely sure, Anne and I agreed that when we got back for the start of a new school year on August 1, I would give it one more month being back in the routine to see if I would feel any different.

The feelings did not change that month. The Lord was clearly leading me to let go of the church I have loved and poured most of my adult life into serving. The time was now. God was leading me to step out in faith and obey his will. Not to do so would be disobedience. So, in September 2018, I shared with the elders that God was leading us to implement our plan for succession.

Chapter 7

IMPLEMENTING THE PLAN

Meeting with the Elders

In the fall of 2018, I met with the elders to tell them I believed God was leading me to implement the process of finding my successor. They were not shocked. They were, however, surprised at the timing. They knew of my desire to keep at it until I was seventy. This was still three years away. We all knew it was coming, but all of us were surprised at when. I certainly was, but I had been talking with Anne and a few key pastors I respected over the last year and a half. I had long been thinking and praying on the matter. They had not. So digesting this news would take more time for them. Yet as I shared the process with them and what I had been through over the past year, they could tell I was sure of God's leading and supported me in this calling to follow God's leading.

In that meeting, I shared a game plan for getting the process underway: (1) I would meet with the executive staff and let them know as well. There would be no way we could go to the church later that fall without their knowing all that was going to take place. (2) We needed to form a search team to call a young pastor who had experience as a pastor who could shepherd a church of our size. A track record of someone who has sat in the seat of pastor is always the best predictor of the future. (3) Because I felt the need to search for my successor outside of Johnson Ferry, I felt I owed an explanation to the young teaching pastors on our staff who were now preaching about ten to twelve times a year. One is a young Gen Xer and two are millennials. They are all good preachers, and I felt they needed to hear from me on why I felt we needed to search for a pastor with pastoral experience outside Johnson Ferry.

A track record of someone who has
sat in the seat of pastor is always
the best predictor of the future.

I realize every college or NFL head coach has to have been in many assistant coaching roles before taking the leap to become the head coach. Some make the transition well, and some who are successful defensive and offensive coordinators in football never make it as a head coach when they finally have that opportunity. Even though I did everything I could to prepare these teaching pastors to plant a church or shepherd an established church by including them in executive staff meetings and in elders meetings and budget prep meetings as well as many opportunities to preach, none of them had ever been a pastor. I just felt it would be healthier for them to have that experience as a church planter or as the pastor of a small or medium-size congregation first.

Their spirit in accepting that was good. How they really felt? They would have to tell you themselves. But knowing that they were all good preachers and each one would have a following in the congregation who felt they would be good for the role, I wanted them to know the recommendation I was giving the elders and would later be giving to the search team. The elders agreed with my plan to meet with the executive pastors and the teaching pastors and would begin to pray with me about the people I would recommend to be on the pastor search team.

Meeting with the Executive Staff

For years I had led the staff and the church through four key executive staff ministers. The elders join with me in overseeing the big-picture issues. They provided essential consultation and input on major changes, capital campaigns, and major new ministries of the church. They also set policy, prayed for the sick by request (James 5:13–16) and took part in church discipline cases. They are the final authority on major issues of the church when the church is not in session.

The executive staff carried out my leadership of the church on a day-to-day basis. They not only had the great responsibility of supervising a large number of people on the staff, but they also held great authority to carry out their responsibility. We met every other week for two to four hours. The executive staff was comprised of the business administrator who oversaw the financial and facility operations of the church, the executive pastor of worship and arts; the executive pastor of global ministries (since the role as executive pastor of global ministries touched every ministry in the church with about two thousand teenagers and adults going on seventy to eighty short-term trips to twenty-five to forty nations each year), and finally the executive pastor of programming and education who supervised the largest number of our staff. Those guys made it happen day-to-day at Johnson Ferry. The executive pastor of programming and education was our rookie on the team (and our first millennial) as he had recently followed a man who had been in that role over twenty years. The other three had been in their roles almost thirty years. That's a lot of tenure, trust, and respect over all those years. When I shared the news with them, it was a different response from the elders. There was immediate tension in the room.

Like the elders, they were surprised but not shocked. Unlike the elders, I could instantly see the executive staff was filled with apprehension. After all, they had the most to lose. How would a new young pastor accept them? Would he want to bring his own staff person for the role they had? What would be his leadership style? No doubt, our executive pastor for worship and arts was the most apprehensive. He is outstanding in his field. His choir and orchestra are topflight! His spirit inspired me the most as our contemporary worship became larger than our traditional worship that he leads. He had been incredibly supportive of the worship leader and his bands that led the contemporary service. Yet he knew few millennial pastors are excited about choirs and orchestras in this era of cultural change in worship styles. His was an understandable apprehension.

They were also uneasy that I was asking them to begin to pray and keep this in confidence until I announced to the church in late November of that year. That was two and a half months away. Why then?

Announcement to the Church

God had led me to preach a series that fall on the life of Moses. It is a boatload of leadership lessons from the greatest godly leader in the Old Testament. The series would go for two and a half months, and the last message would be on Moses passing the baton of leadership to Joshua. In that message I would teach how God led Moses to choose Joshua as his successor and then share, as part of that message, that God was leading me to begin the search for my successor.

We also planned to have a video prepared to go on our website that same afternoon where Anne and I could share in more detail how God had led us to this decision. This would allow those who were not there that day to hear directly from Anne and me versus hearing the news from others. You can pull up that sermon and video on right-fromtheheart.org.

The idea of Anne being on the video with me came from a conversation I had with another long-tenured pastor who had retired earlier that year. He told me to figure out the best way for the congregation to hear from my wife. He said,

"Since you have pastored there for thirty-seven years, your wife's perspective on God's leading in this process will be enormous in helping them see how God has led throughout this time." This made sense to me. Anne and I have been a team in ministry. He also added, "It would help the congregation to better accept that God was really leading in this decision if they see you both together about God's leading." It was great advice. That video would make a huge difference in the process.

In both the sermon and the video, I shared that I would be bringing a recommended pastor search team to the church for their approval in January 2019. I asked them to pray for me while building that team and of course to pray for us all in the days ahead.

So now the word was out. The only pastor Johnson Ferry had ever known was retiring. I was thankful it was finally public. The last two and a half months of sitting on that announcement with Anne and the church leaders had not been easy. The year 2019 was going to be an important year for Johnson Ferry.

Chapter 8

THE SEARCH TEAM

Once the announcement was made in late November 2018, I spent the month of December prayerfully seeking to build a search team to present to the elders for their approval. Then the team would be presented to the congregation in mid-January 2019 for their approval.

In the fall leading up to my announcement, the elders also felt strongly that it would be wise to employ a search firm to assess, lead, and offer guidance in the process. They knew I had collected more than thirty names of outstanding young pastors over the last few years, but they felt we owed it to the church to hire a search firm to conduct a national search and leave no stone uncovered. So, even though we looked at several firms, we were unanimous in going with Vanderbloemen.

The founder, William Vanderbloemen, had been such a help to us when we were working through our succession plan a few years earlier. He assigned us an outstanding consultant that had served for many years on a megachurch staff and specialized in pastor searches for large churches. It was helpful to begin to talk with the consultant and seek his counsel behind the scenes before the announcement was made, along with my prayerful process of thinking through who should be on the search team. These are some of the insights he shared: (1) Don't make it too large. It makes coming to a decision difficult. (2) Seek people who have wisdom about leadership, your church's culture, and the respect of their peers. (3) Seek out people who will and can make time for what will be a demanding process. An occasional attender to the meetings can muddy up the process with uninformed insight. (4) Be sure you have a strong and capable chairman and cochairman who can keep the process going, someone who is widely known and respected by the congregation. I shared with him that finding the chairman of the search team had become a major focus of my prayers.

At Johnson Ferry we are blessed with several elders who have served multiple terms as elders. Since they are selected by the congregation to serve three-year terms, then rotating off for at least one year, it had become obvious who the most respected leaders were.

Two of those elders kept coming to my mind. One was a partner with one of the largest executive search firms in the world that focus on C-suite executives of Fortune 500 companies and major university presidential searches. He is also a respected Bible teacher and even filled the pulpit for me from time to time. The other was a partner in one of the big four accounting firms and recently led the search for a new headmaster of one of Atlanta's most prominent Christian schools while serving as chairman of the board of that school. It was intriguing that the search he led for a new school headmaster was for a person to follow a long-tenured headmaster who had been successful in building that school. In other words, they searched for someone to come and build on a strong foundation of a healthy, kindergarten through twelfth grade Christian school. The similarities of that situation to Johnson Ferry were clear.

As I continued to pray about who God was leading to be chairman of the search team, I kept going to those two elders. Eventually, I felt led to approach them both about being cochairmen. I had worked with them for many years in leading Johnson Ferry Baptist Church. They were well-respected spiritual leaders in Johnson Ferry and knew our church culture well. Probably just as important, they had worked well together as elders for many years. All those thoughts would prove true in the months ahead as they served in the leadership role together.

The Members of the Search Team

For years Johnson Ferry had been a baby boomer-lead congregation. It was founded by boomers who called a founding pastor who is a boomer, led by an executive staff of boomers, along with elders who were overwhelmingly boomers (with a few Gen Xers sprinkled in from time to time). For Johnson Ferry to find a gifted millennial or younger Gen X age pastor, we needed the search team to have a good representation of boomers, Gen Xers, and millennials. With both our cochairman being younger boomers, that meant the majority of the rest of the committee needed to be Gen Xers or millennials.

We also needed representation of women. Johnson Ferry believes in the biblical leadership model of men as elders and deacons along with a complementarian model of men as spiritual leaders in their home (1 Tim. 3:1–13; Eph. 5:22–33). Because of this biblical teaching, so many men in Johnson Ferry know that their calling is to lead like Jesus—to be servant leaders in the home. Thus, women and wives within the church body have filled our church with many strong women leaders. How can this be? Culture would expect just the opposite. Hollywood, the media, corporate culture, and theologically liberal churches would tend to think it would be just the opposite. But when men lead with Christlike servant leadership, women soar. Women have been chairpersons of key committees in our church like the finance, budget prep, and personnel committee multiple times. Some of our strongest adult Bible teachers within the church are women. In addition to these, many of the Johnson Ferry women are key leaders in their chosen profession in the workplace.

But when men lead with Christlike servant leadership, women soar.

I also felt that one of the weaknesses of our congregation had always been our lack of ethnic diversity. A big part of that has been the local mission field where God has planted us in North Atlanta. The congregation largely reflects the makeup of our community, which is overwhelmingly Anglo. Even though Atlanta is known as the "Black Mecca" of all America's major cities, the largest ethnic group in our upper middle-class community is Asian followed by a smaller percentage of African American and even smaller percentage of Hispanics. But in recent years those percentages have been changing dramatically, and to reach our community in the future, we needed a search committee who were sensitive to that.

These things were on my mind as I prayed about who should be on the search team. But even more important than all these issues was finding the right person who would seek God's will in the process. We did not need or want people who would push a preconceived agenda of the type of person they wanted to be our next pastor. This has always been true of our elders; they are and have been men who are most of all seeking God's will for Johnson Ferry. I thank the Lord that He has protected us from agenda-driven elders, and I prayed that the Lord would protect us from agenda-driven search team members.

I also hoped and prayed that the search team would be able to come to a unanimous recommendation, and the best chance for that happening is for mature Christians to seek God's will and not what they feel is best. This could not be compromised.

The search team I was led to recommend was comprised of six men and four women. Four were boomers including the two chairmen, three were Gen Xers, and three were millennials. One boomer woman was an African American, and one Gen Xer was Asian American. All members of the search committee were well-respected among their peers. Amazingly, every person I reached out to about serving agreed to serve. Then, when the group was presented to the elders (with the endorsement of the two cochairmen), the elders unanimously endorsed them.

In January 2019, they were presented to the congregation for the church's approval. Because the church was asked to pray diligently from the time of the announcement for God's leading on the search team, the church came spiritually ready when the group was presented. And because few in the church would know all of them, we prepared a brief bio of each person with their picture on the screen and which generation they represented.

Amazingly, the church unanimously approved the search team in all six Sunday morning services. God clearly had His hand on the process. Now the hard work would begin.

Chapter 9

THE SEARCH TEAM PROCESS

When the search team was approved, they did not immediately begin the search process. The church members began to bring forth names for them to consider. The search committee kept them all on file for nearly two months. Important preparation for that search process needed to come first.

Preparation: The Consultant

Our consultant immediately began to get to know the culture of Johnson Ferry. Before he thought about candidates to bring to the search committee, he wanted to know who Johnson Ferry is. He met with the elders, the executive staff, the search team cochairmen, the search team as a whole, and other key leaders in the church.

He and his team attended worship services and worked with our executive staff on obtaining key information about the church. The mission and core values, theological beliefs (especially on hot button issues), the church's history, the ministries God had clearly blessed, church families, and on and on. If there was something to know about our church, the consultant would find it. The work his team did over the first few weeks really grasped the church culture of Johnson Ferry. This helped the Vanderbloemen team develop a profile of the type of candidates that would be a good fit for our church culture.

Prayer

We asked the church to pray. Our prayer ministry mobilized with continual prayer that God would lead in this process. In the first meetings of the search team, there was a major focus on praying together.

Team Building

Bringing together ten people who mostly did not know one another well, if at all, from three generations in the church was a key priority. They needed to get to know one another, to hear one another's story of how Jesus transformed their lives, their experience in Johnson Ferry, and what their hopes were for the future pastor and the church. That did not occur in one meeting. It took time.

Research

In the meantime, I gave the cochairman and the search consultant the more than thirty names of young pastors that I had been collecting for almost five years. Some were on the list from the beginning. Some were recently added from the two new mentoring groups of young pastors I led over a two-year period. I had some preferences but did not share who those were. As I mentioned earlier, members and friends of the church were also submitting names from the time I announced that our search for my successor was beginning. The

Vanderbloemen Company was also doing research on its vast reservoir of names from all over the nation. They researched extensively every name they received. The hours the consulting staff gives to this part of the vetting of names and prospects would take a pastor search team of volunteers six months to a year to complete. The search firm did all this in just a few months. That would make it a much shorter process than we at Johnson Ferry expected.

My Role as Pastor

I believed that the search team needed to discern God's will on who our next pastor would be. But I also trusted the Holy Spirit to move in all of us to confirm that decision. I shared with the two cochairmen that the one request I had was that as they begin to zero in on a prospect, if I did not feel right about the candidate, they would not call that person. They completely agreed. It has always amazed me—really dumbfounded me—that churches with long-tenured pastors usually leave the retiring pastor out of the process. No one in the congregation knows the church like a long-tenured pastor, and certainly no one in the congregation can grasp the challenges a new pastor is going to face like the pastor of that church. So I was in the search team meetings but mostly as an observer. I observed the individual members of the search team as they began to look at specific candidates but usually did not participate unless I was asked a question. There were times after meetings were over when the two cochairmen and I would discuss the process more deeply.

No one in the congregation knows the church like a long-tenured pastor, and certainly no one in the congregation can grasp the challenges a new pastor is going to face like the pastor of that church.

Some meetings I did not attend, especially when the search team began to share what they were hoping for in a new pastor. All pastors have strengths, weaknesses, and limitations. The search team needed to be able to speak freely with one another and the consultant without worrying that they might hurt my feelings. They did not want to touch on hopes for a new pastor that I might perceive as criticism.

Zeroing in on Top Candidates

After several months of prayer and research—where more than one hundred candidates were considered and vetted, the consultant brought the recommendations of nine candidates to the search team. Each candidate was open to being considered, but none of them were committed in any way to come if called. They were all simply open to praying and discussing the possibility. Each of them had also been asked to prepare a brief video with their wives to introduce themselves by sharing some of their story and their insight on pastoring a church. This helped the search team have a starting point of considering serious candidates. The whole search team watched all of the videos together without comment. They took notes and waited to the end of the process to see if God might be leading them to pursue specific questions and discussions with any or some of them later.

The consultant was clear. If the search team was not led to talk further with any of the candidates, they would start the process over with more candidates. He was simply starting with those nine that he felt had the most potential to be a good fit for Johnson Ferry. After these videos, the search team had access to several sermons from each of the candidates to view on their own in the coming days. This was the beginning of an intensive time for the search team. They would have to give many hours to the process now. After the search team had watched the sermon videos, they met and showed interest in interviewing six of the nine.

Video Interviews

The consultant set up interviews via video for all six of the candidates. They met by conference call with three candidates each night for two long meetings. Each interview was about one hour in length.

I did not know four of the candidates who were brought to us by our consultant. Two were candidates from the thirty plus names I had given to the search team and the consultant when the process began.

It was fascinating to sit in on those interviews. All six were gifted and capable pastors who were being blessed where they were currently serving. Because they were all so gifted, I was thankful that the consultant who had led in preparation for all this would be the one to eventually tell five of the six that Johnson Ferry would be going with someone else. Yet at the same time, it was obvious that each candidate was seeking God's will and would trust how God opens and closes doors as we all were seeking His will.

At the end of those two long nights of interviews, God seemed to be leading one candidate to the forefront of the six. (I could just sense that candidate really connected with the search team.) I did not say anything to the team about what I was perceiving at the time. Yet God seemed to be all over one particular interview. I do, however, remember asking our most senior member of the search team (who is one of Johnson Ferry's charter members and in the early days of Johnson Ferry served for ten years as my executive assistant) what she thought as we finished the two nights of interviews. She looked at me and smiled and said, "I've got no doubt who it is." Without either one of us saying the name, we both knew what the other was thinking. It was just so obvious how things clicked in that interview.

Insights Will Now Be Included from My Successor: Clay Smith

Clay: In the fall of 2018, I was heading into my fifth year as the senior pastor of First Baptist Church of Matthews, North Carolina (a suburb of Charlotte). God had blessed our church with substantial growth and vitality. One of our major issues was a lack of parking, as our church only owned five acres in a downtown historic district. I reached out to an old college friend and fraternity brother, George Wright, who was the new pastor at Shandon Baptist in Columbia, South Carolina. Not only did I know George, but I had served at Shandon for six years prior to moving to Charlotte. George mentioned that his dad, Bryant Wright, had dealt with similar land limitations at Johnson Ferry Baptist Church in the Atlanta area and that I should reach out to him to learn more.

A few weeks later, Bryant and I had a long phone call. I was impressed with his candor, knowledge, and wisdom. He told me about Johnson Ferry, and I was excited to learn more about him and his church. Bryant invited me to participate in a mentoring group he would be leading for pastors of medium-size churches similar to ours. He had apparently been conducting these groups for a number of years. I looked at the proposed dates for Bryant's group and wrote him my regrets, as I could not make it work. I had been elected president of the Baptist State of North Carolina board of directors that year, and my time availability was already limited. Bryant responded by telling me of a second mentoring group for pastors from larger churches and invited me to take part in that one instead. Little did I know that saying yes to that invitation would bring about a tremendous change to my life.

At our first meeting, I quickly discovered that every pastor in the group except me had followed a long-tenured pastor at a large church. It was fascinating to hear each of the five men describe their experiences, frustrations, and victories while transitioning into such a role. But I was on the outside looking in, as that was not my experience. We concluded the first meeting, and while our current professional situations were different, I was grateful for the new friends I had made. I went about my life, seeking God's direction for where He wanted to take our church in Charlotte.

One month later I found myself sitting in a restaurant having lunch with a potential ministerial candidate for our church staff when my phone rang. The caller ID read "Bryant Wright," and I let the call go to voicemail. After lunch I called him back, and Bryant gave me some meaningful affirmation and shared the news that he had submitted my name, along with several others, to the search group they were using to find his replacement. I was honored that he'd consider me, but I did not think seriously about the fact that it might actually happen. Other churches had called me through the years, but I had turned them all down. We were happy in Charlotte and thriving in the church to which God had called us.

Two weeks later I received word from Vanderbloemen Search Group that my name had been given to them by a number of pastors who had recommended me for Johnson Ferry. Pastors have different philosophies on how to handle these recommendations and phone calls from potential churches. I'm of the opinion that you should at least consider all of them since you never know when God might be calling you to a new work. Besides, if it becomes a clear no, either through personal prayer or through the church going in a different direction, it typically reaffirms your commitment to your current church. So, it's a win-win. I submitted my answers to their questions, and they said they would be in touch. I didn't hear anything for three weeks, but I began to pray and ask God for His clear will and direction in my life. My heart was not looking to leave, but I was open to whatever He wanted.

I received a phone call from the Vanderbloemen Group, saying they wanted me to meet in person with the consultant leading the search. I flew to Nashville, Tennessee, and met with Tim Stevens, vice president of Consulting, in the airport. We talked for two hours about my family, call to ministry, current church, and future aspirations. Tim was easy to talk to, and I enjoyed getting to know him. The irony that we met right beside an area in the airport called the Wright Business Center did not go unnoticed. Tim told me at the end of that meeting that I would be one of the finalists he would recommend to the Johnson Ferry pastor search team. In the meantime, he asked me to make a six-minute video with Terrica, my wife, telling them about my call to ministry, my heart for missions, and how I would lead a church the size of Johnson Ferry. We filmed the video in our den and sent it off to Vanderbloemen.

A week or so later, I received a call from Tim, letting me know that the Johnson Ferry search team wanted to schedule a virtual meeting with me. In that meeting, they stated that I was one of six candidates they were talking to and wanted to spend about an hour getting to know me and my approach to pastoral ministry. I don't remember all of their exact questions, but they ranged from how I planned my preaching to my favorite three books of all time to my hobbies on the weekend. Because the camera they used did not capture the whole room, I asked if they could pass the computer from one person to the next so I could "meet" each one. Remember, I was also interviewing them. They passed the computer around, and we laughed a lot about how clumsy we all felt in doing so. All in all, it was a good talk, and they seemed like people I'd like to get to know better.

I received a call from John Farish, one of the cochairs of the Johnson Ferry search team, telling me how much they enjoyed our conversation and that they would like to meet me in person. He also expressed that I was now one of three candidates they were considering. These can be awkward conversations, as you feel a little bit like you're in a horse race but don't know whom you're racing against, nor can you see the finish line. I was praying daily to God to make sure my motives were pure and that I was following His will. Terrica and I adopted Psalm 143:8–10 as our prayer focus during the search. The psalmist talks about experiencing God's love, asking for God to show His will, protection from enemies, and the ability to do what He asks us to do. I boiled those down to four key thoughts: "God, remind me that You love me no matter what, show me what we should do in this, keep me from internal and external enemies that want to drown out Your voice, and give me the courage and know-how to walk into your will for my life."

Evaluations of the Interviews

Bryant: Once the interviews were completed, they were followed by several days of prayer by the search team. Then they got back together and zeroed in on two of the candidates they wanted to get to know personally. They also wanted to visit their churches and see them in person. In addition to that, the cochairmen would invite those two candidates to Johnson Ferry for a visit on our campus. This took a few weeks to coordinate and fulfill all the travel plans, for not only were the two pastors men who had busy schedules, but the members of the search team are all busy folks with families. At the same time, it was a lot easier for two or three at a time to slip into the candidates' worship services versus a group of ten walking in together. That would be impossible to be discreet and unnoticed.

I had one concern. One of the six candidates that they didn't feel led to continue discussions with had been one of my recommendations. Before the process of interviews and sermon videos took place, I felt that there was a good possibility he was God's man. As the interviews took place, it was obvious things didn't click with the search team like I thought they might. So I asked the cochairmen if I could personally break the news to him because Anne and I love him and his wife. He is such a gifted young pastor. And since he knew I had given the search team his name, I felt like I needed to be the one to tell him that the Lord was not leading the search team in his direction. He was disappointed but gracious in receiving the news.

Clay: A few weeks later, I flew to Atlanta by myself for a full slate of meetings with team members from Johnson Ferry. I ate dinner with the two cochairs, John Farish and George Ethridge. We talked about the process, what it's like to live in the Atlanta area, and the history of Johnson Ferry. We then drove over to the church so that I could walk around and see the place. It was 9:00 p.m. or so, but I was surprised by how many people were still in the building. John and George were sneaking me around corners so as not to be seen. It was secret, but we were laughing the whole time. The next morning I had breakfast with Bryant and Anne at their house. Anne cooked a delicious meal with bacon, eggs, grits, and the works. We talked about family, ministry, and how things were going overall. Bryant and I then continued the conversation in his home study, talking mainly through theology. He wanted to know, for example, my view on the Bible, my view on soteriology, my view on gender roles in ministry, etc. I love talking about these things so it was enjoyable. We talked for two hours but only had time to cover half the subjects.

George Ethridge picked me up and drove me to the church where I would meet with the Johnson Ferry search team. Since there were ten on the team, they decided the best way for us to get to know each other was to have two ninety-minute meetings back to back. Half of the members were in each meeting. We exchanged questions, and I found the meetings to be productive. My friendship was growing with each member of the search team, and our connection was deepening. The second group meeting ended, and I was whisked off to the airport to fly back to Charlotte. My mind and heart were both shifting from "what if" to "this may actually happen."

Pastoral transitions are tough. As my heart and mind started to shift to serving in Atlanta, I was also grieving for the people I love in

Charlotte. They were family to me, and I thought I would serve there for much longer than five years. Johnson Ferry is a great church, and many from the outside looking in might think such a decision would be easy. But the fact of the matter is that leaving Charlotte would be one of the hardest decisions of my life. Our three girls had great friends. They loved their schools. We were heavily involved in our community and were part of a great revival of sorts at First Baptist Matthews. Why would God move us? Why now? These are the types of thoughts that circled my mind constantly. There is nothing harder than trying to lead with a divided heart. You feel like you're cheating on your spouse and keeping a bad secret. At the same time, I was growing more and more excited with what was happening at Johnson Ferry, and I started to think seriously about what it could look like to be used by God there.

Our main prayer after each leg of the search was, "God, do you want us to go to the next step?" We felt nothing but affirmation with each stage of the search process. The Johnson Ferry team let me know that they had released their other candidates and were now talking only to me. This was now officially serious. The next step was a full slate of meetings in which Terrica and I would meet with the personnel team and the elders. Instead of flying, we decided to drive to Atlanta. The drive took over four hours, so it was a long day. It was also Vacation Bible School week at our church in Charlotte, one of the busiest and most pivotal times of the year. I imagine our leave caused a few raised eyebrows when I took it as a vacation day and Terrica got a substitute to lead her VBS group. We drove to Atlanta and shared our story in a string of separate meetings with the personnel team, the elders, and the executive staff of the church. After the meetings, we made the long trek back home and arrived around midnight. We were exhausted, but this was all part of the process.

The next step was a phone call with Tim Stevens at Vanderbloemen. The call would focus on my desired compensation. Pastors approach these conversations in different ways. Some say they will gladly receive whatever the church offers. I, however, have always found it important to have this conversation. That is not to say that I would go to the church because of money. But I would also not want money to be the reason I wouldn't go to Johnson Ferry. God's call is not threatened by doing my due diligence to investigate the circumstances to which I would be entering. Tim Stevens asked me to think of answers to the following two questions: What would I *need* to have, and what would be *nice* to have? He was not only asking about salary but about other requests in compensation that might help me effectively do my job. I came up with a list of reasonable requests and submitted them to Tim. He then talked these over with the pastor search team cochairs, and they called me to agree to the terms. I should also say that the final compensation number was not arbitrarily picked out of the air. Johnson Ferry had done extensive research to determine appropriate compensation ranges that reflect churches of similar size, the scope of ministry, and cost of living in North Atlanta.

The next step in the interview process was to make a final visit to Johnson Ferry with our entire family. This would be a trip for Terrica and me to meet with the entire search team on Saturday night, attend church on Sunday morning, and have one last time with the search team on Sunday afternoon. We had a previously scheduled trip to

Birmingham, Alabama, to attend the annual meeting of the Southern Baptist Convention so I was already planning not to preach that Sunday. We had not yet told our three daughters what was in the works. Given their ages, we didn't think they would be able to keep this a secret. More importantly, we did not want them to experience the roller coaster of emotions if we or the team decided not to take this journey to its intended destination. We told our kids that we were stopping by Atlanta on the way to visit the church of my "pastor mentor," Bryant Wright. Pastors' kids are used to being shuffled to and from churches and church conferences, so this wasn't that big of a deal to them. We had a great dinner that night and attended two different services on Sunday morning. It was funny because the search team could not be seen with us in order not to reveal any acquaintance. So we would see them in the hall and instinctively wave, but they would only secretly wave back with a nod of the head or some other subtle gesture. It was like a game of hide-and-seek. We found it amusing. Our favorite part of the morning was the last worship service. The Johnson Ferry student choir had just returned from a mission trip to New

York City and was presenting their concert to the church. It was awesome and our kids loved it. To see that many young people praising Jesus was awe-inspiring.

The Decision

Bryant: As the process continued to unfold and the search committee had zeroed in on two prospects, it was fascinating to hear each member speak and see that the search team was not unanimous at this point. Both men were strong candidates. But it was also clear that one candidate was emerging as the favorite of the two. The team agreed that some of them would make another visit to see them in action.

Then, as the cochairmen continued discussing with the individuals on the team and the search team got back together a couple of weeks later, they were now sure that God was leading Clay Smith to be our next pastor.

I was not surprised. Ever since they had first interviewed Clay by video, I too felt God was leading us to him. After that initial interview, I watched Clay's sermons. They were so good that I was absolutely sure he was God's man.

So, when the search team came together to make a decision, each person spoke. It was clear as they went around the room that they were now unanimous. They voted to issue a call to Clay contingent on the church's approval. Then one of our cochairmen asked me to pray. Suddenly I was flooded with emotion—so much so that I couldn't speak. No words would come out. I was overwhelmed with how God guided the process and how clearly God had led us all. But I was also overwhelmed with gratitude that the Lord had had His powerful hand on our church for thirty-seven and a half years, and He had given me the privilege to be her founding pastor all that time. Yet, most of all, I was overwhelmed that the time had really come. The time of letting go of the church I loved, helped birth, poured my heart and life into for thirty-seven and a half years had arrived. After a long tearful moment of silence, I finally began to pray. That prayer took a while to get through.

Tears are flowing over again in writing these words as I reflect on how God moved so powerfully and so clearly in a group of believers seeking God's will. It is one of those rare times in life when you know you are standing on holy ground. The greatness of God was so evident in that moment that words just would not come. It was a holy moment indeed! God had moved. A new day was coming. Life would never be the same for any of us!

Chapter 10

THE SUCCESSOR IS INTRODUCED

Bryant: Once the search team came to a unanimous decision with the full support of Anne and me, the cochairs visited with Clay and Terrica with the news. Of course, any calling of God involves both parties. At this point in the process, I feel it will be most helpful to hear from Clay and let him speak on how God led him in the process.

Clay: We left the church and had lunch with the search team. We answered a few more questions and shared our impressions of worship. With that, we said our goodbyes, and the team stayed behind to hold a vote. It was odd to drive away from a house, knowing that the ten people inside were talking about us and voting on our future. We enjoyed getting to know them, and God was uniting our hearts together. We had little doubt that they were feeling as excited as we were. We received a call a few hours later as we pulled into Birmingham, telling us that the team had unanimously voted to recommend me as the second pastor of Johnson Ferry. Terrica and I were both thrilled and nervous. We were excited about entering into the great legacy of leadership at Johnson Ferry. But we also knew this meant that our time at First Baptist Church Matthews was coming to an end. We were heartbroken at the thought of telling people we dearly loved that God had given us a new assignment. But more than anything, we were confident that God had created this opportunity, and we were obedient to what He wanted us to do. That's all that really matters in the end.

The Cochairmen Met with Clay and Terrica

Bryant: First, the cochairmen shared the exciting news of a unanimous decision to extend the call to Clay as the next senior pastor of Johnson Ferry. Second, they came up with a salary package (along with our personnel chairman who was on the search team)—that included salary and detailed benefits to offer to Clay. This was done in coordination with the consultant, the personnel committee, the cochairmen, and me. With the long tenure of some of our key executive staff and ministerial staff, they had excellent salaries for a job well done over many years of ministry. Still, it is essential that the senior pastor be the highest paid person on the church staff despite his age or limited years of experience as a pastor. At the same time, they felt that his salary at forty years old should not be equal to a senior pastor of a megachurch like Johnson Ferry that had served thirty-seven years and was sixty-seven years old. Still, we all felt that it needed to be a generous offer that allowed for growth over the years and included all the benefits I had received as pastor of Johnson Ferry. Then they gave Clay and Terrica a few days to pray and suggest any adjustments they felt were appropriate. Thankfully, Clay confirmed how God was leading them and accepted the call.

The Announcement to the Church

When the decision on Clay was made in June 2019, our hope was to announce it to the church in mid-July and tell the church that he would be coming to preach in view of a call on the first Sunday of August (the weekend our public schools began a new academic year). That Sunday is always a big day for the church as people who have been away on summer vacations are back home. July is our most down month of church attendance as the schools in our district have squeezed the summer from basically three to two months over the years and begin the new year around August 1 versus after Labor Day (which I think is crazy, but that editorial opinion is irrelevant to this book). July was also my annual vacation break as pastor. So we discussed whether I would need to come back from vacation on the Sunday of the announcement as a show of support. Because we then had five services with two styles of worship and I had alternated venues each Sunday (when I preached in person in one venue, the other venue saw my preaching the message via video), we all felt it would be no problem for me to share my endorsement of the search teams decision for Clay via video. We also felt that the video needed to include me, Clay, and Terrica. So the arrangement was made to film that endorsement with Clay and

Terrica standing with me. He and Terrica shared their excitement about his coming to be our new pastor. This would be shown on the Sunday of the announcement of whom the search team was unanimously recommending as Johnson Ferry's new pastor.

The Influence of Social Media

In this day of instant news, we had to consider social media. It is no longer possible for a potential pastor to go preach in view of a call to another church and then, if approved, announce his new calling to the church where he is presently serving. Today, news is instantly shared over social media. This means the pastor coming in view of a call must announce his new calling simultaneously to the church where he is presently pastoring.

So that day our two cochairmen made the announcement about Clay Smith to Johnson Ferry while Clay was sharing his call to Johnson Ferry to his congregation in Charlotte. We felt it was better for each cochairman to share this announcement live in our two venues. They used basically the same script that explained the search process and how the search team came to unanimous recommendation of Clay. Then each of them introduced the video of me endorsing Clay and Terrica and the both of them sharing their excitement.

Worshipping Online

Two major changes have occurred in church life over the last ten to fifteen years. One is giving online, which allows people to give faithfully whether they are in attendance or not. It makes the gifts in the offering plate seem small, and some of our ushers and deacons collecting the offering in worship sometimes have people silently mouth to them when the plate is passed, "I give online." This trend has had a dramatic impact for good on giving of tithes and offerings to the church. In the past, when regular givers were away, many did not catch up on giving for the Sundays they were absent. This would become hugely important to churches during the Covid pandemic. But in Johnson Ferry, with more than 60 percent of all gifts given online, there is a greater consistency in giving among regular givers.

The second major change in worship is streaming our services online. This allows the members and attenders to join in worship while they are away. This also became incredibly important during Covid. Even though July might seem to be the worst month of the year to make this announcement, with online viewing, everyone could hear the announcement at the same time versus through word of mouth. We promoted the date of the announcement, and the search team, elders, and executive staff were sworn to secrecy. We did not want word to reach the church Clay was pastoring before he had a chance to tell them in person.

Thankfully, word didn't leak. If it had because of social media, the whole world would have quickly known. As you can imagine, our online viewing of Johnson Ferry worship was off the charts that day. It was four times what we normally had on a Sunday. I remember gathering with my extended family at the beach and watching the announcement all together. I imagine the excitement we all felt was similar to what Johnson Ferry folks watching online from all over the country were feeling that day as God was beginning a new chapter in our church history.

Clay Coming to Preach in View of a Call

Once the word was out, the next big step was prepping for Clay to come and preach on August 4 when he and his family would be introduced in person to the congregation. This would also be my opportunity to speak in person to the church and take part in the introduction of Clay that day. It was an emotional day for all of us. Excitement and anticipation were high, as you would expect. Clay preached an outstanding message, and it was clear in every service that God was moving. I could tell he was connecting with our people, and they were connecting with him.

Clay: I was officially called as the second senior pastor of Johnson Ferry on August 4, 2019, after preaching in all five Sunday morning worship services. My preaching text was Hebrews 12:1–3 with a message I entitled "Start to Finish." I talked about the need for endurance in the pastorate and in the Christian life in general. I made a remark that had more staying power than I had planned. I mentioned that many well-meaning people, after hearing of my new call, would say, "Wow, those are big shoes to fill." I replied, "I'm not here to fill

Bryant's shoes; I'm here to fill mine." I said this not to disrespect Bryant or belittle his almost forty years of faithful service but to convey that God did not call me to Johnson Ferry to be Bryant Wright. He called me to be Clay Smith. One of the great pieces of advice I received early in ministry was to be myself. God gave me specific talents, opportunities, and experiences from which to learn. The greatest gift I could give Johnson Ferry was to be the healthiest version of me. So I was not there to fill Bryant's shoes.

I preached three times that Sunday morning, which was broadcast in multiple venues across five services. After each sermon I was whisked out of the worship center, and the congregation would vote on the recommendation from the elders and search team to call me as pastor. It was a unanimous vote in all five services, and on August 4, 2019, I was officially called as the second senior pastor of Johnson Ferry.

Bryant: As Clay was speaking, I was filled with gratitude to God for guiding us so clearly in the search process. And once again I was overwhelmed with thankfulness to the Lord for being able to pastor Johnson Ferry for thirty-seven and a half years. God had blessed us so amazingly. Now He was blessing us again with an outstanding young pastor to lead the church in a new day.

But it was doubly emotional for me, for my father—my hero—the finest Christian man I've ever known was at the point of death. Our family had been gathered at his bedside during that week, knowing that the end of his life on earth was eminent. Anne got the call that he graduated to heaven right at the beginning of the third service that day. What a mixture of emotions. I was about to stand up to introduce our new pastor when I heard that my dad had graduated to heaven. I didn't want to say anything to the congregation about his passing for this was a great day for our church and Clay and Terrica. But amazingly, as God does in times like that, He allowed me to keep my emotions in check and take part in the service with great joy.

As I listened to Clay preach from Hebrews 12:1–3, feeling tremendous joy that he was clearly God's man ("Therefore, since we also have such a large cloud of witnesses surrounding us"), I was overwhelmed with tears of gratitude that my dad— one of the finest adult Bible study teachers in our church—had a bird's-eye view of this great day in the life of our church. He died of Alzheimer's, and thoughts of him leaning over the balcony of heaven in sound mind cheering us on overwhelmed me. He had always been my greatest encourager as he was to countless hundreds who knew him.

Clay was unanimously called to be our new pastor on the day my dad stepped into the presence of the Lord. It was a great day for Johnson Ferry, a great day for Clay and Terrica, and an even greater day for my dad who was now in the "cloud of witnesses" in heaven rejoicing with us!

Chapter 11

THE SUCCESSION BEGINS

When Clay was unanimously called to be our pastor on August 4, we told the congregation that he would begin preaching on September 5. We also told them that Clay and I would share the preaching load for about three months in a transition period. Since we did this together, Clay and I are writing this chapter together as well.

We gave a month to Clay and Terrica to have some time off to move from Charlotte to Atlanta and get settled in. In reality, it turned into about one week. The Charlotte school system is much wiser than our public schools in Metro Atlanta, and they begin the new academic year around Labor Day (as God intended). This meant that Clay and Terrica had to get their three daughters settled into new schools almost right away, or they would move here a month behind in school. So what was planned as a three-month overlap became closer to four months. Clay was not interested in living here and not getting started at Johnson Ferry.

Clay: Bryant and the elders had recommended that I spend a good bit of August taking personal time to move and recharge my batteries. While I appreciated the gesture, it proved impractical. Public schools in Cobb County started on August 1. We had to move ASAP to get our three girls enrolled in their schools. God provided in many ways during that period, namely, in another local church allowing us to stay in one of their mission houses rent-free for a few months. I so appreciated the kingdom mindset of that pastor and am indebted to his generosity.

Bryant: One thing Clay pointed out to others in why our transition time was going so well is how important communication is. We began meeting for a couple of hours weekly to talk about Johnson Ferry, ministry, staff, key leaders, and big challenges ahead for the church and anything on our mind. These meetings quickly became the highlight of my week. You know you are enjoying working with someone when at the end of each meeting you feel there are a dozen things you want to talk about and didn't get to. We really connected.

We also went over clarity of a game plan in scheduling these steps of the handoff: sermon series we would preach together, meetings and ministries he would need to attend, really anything on the schedule. In most cases if we were at an event or meeting together, I would lead it so he could see my approach and have an idea of how things were being done, and then we would debrief about this in our weekly meeting. In addition to that, I shared with him the dates of when I felt he ought to be leading versus me for things like executive staff, all staff, elders, deacons, etc. Sometimes I would be there to see him in action, and we would debrief about those meetings on our weekly check-ins. But in the second half of this transition, Clay would be leading the meetings without my being there. This way the staff and key leaders of ministry in the church could literally see a transition taking place right before their eyes—symbolically and literally.

Also, on this schedule was a clear end date for me to complete my time as pastor. It seems that so many problems in the succession transition occur not only because of poor communication and expectations but because the retiring pastor or minister or company CEO is too vague with his successor and the people on when the end date is. Once there was clarity on the end date, we were able to finalize series we would preach together, and the church was able to decide on an appreciation day for Anne and me a few weeks before my final Sunday on December 15, 2019—exactly thirty-eight years from when I began as the founding pastor of Johnson Ferry Baptist Church on December 15, 1981.

Clay: Bryant and I copastored Johnson Ferry for a period of four months. This was new for both of us and proved awkward at times. After all, with both of us sitting at the table, who was in charge? Fortunately, we mapped out a detailed plan for the entire period down to who would lead each meeting and when we would complete the transition. For example, with four scheduled elder meetings during that overlap time, Bryant led the first two, and I led the last two.

We did the same with all of the pastoral responsibilities even down to birth and bereavement letters. If a baby were born to a family in the church, they received a letter from me since I would be their pastor going forward. In the case of a death, Bryant sent a letter to the family since he had been their pastor. We did the same for preaching. We overlapped for seventeen Sundays and mapped out the series together, along with who would preach each sermon. This was fun. As someone who was used to preaching every week, I appreciated the break, which allowed for more margin during the week to meet new faces and connect with the people of Johnson Ferry.

Bryant: Clay arrived to preach his first sermon as our new pastor on September 8. I had moved out of the pastor's office so he could move into it. It was just another symbol that there was "a new sheriff in town." During that interim time I used an upstairs study where I did sermon prep for years and occasionally had meetings with people in unused office space at the time.

In discussing key staff, I made clear to everyone that each person serves on the staff by the decision of the pastor and that would be true for whoever succeeded me. A pastor who doesn't have the authority and freedom to do so will never really be the pastor of the church.

At the same time, Clay was coming into a healthy church with a gifted and long-tenured staff. The search team, our consultant, and I shared with Clay that he would have complete freedom on building his staff. And yet this was not a church in crisis with a bunch of staff that needed to go because the previous pastor didn't fulfill his leadership responsibilities. In the days leading up to Clay's call as senior pastor, two critical openings occurred on our staff. Our long-tenured business administrator of about thirty years retired. Right before that, our long-tenured student pastor was called to be the university pastor of Samford University. Since these occurred while we were in the process of our search for a senior pastor, I felt that their replacements from within the staff would take on the title of "interim." I felt it would not be fair to the successor to fill those key roles versus his doing it himself. This would give the new pastor a great opportunity to begin to build a team where he made the decision on whom to call to be on his team.

Clay: The most meaningful thing we did together during our overlap was something we called the "Great Commission Offering." Bryant felt led to ask the church to give to the Great Commission as a final act of his pastorate. The initial goal was $3 million dollars on one day, which was to be divided among the Southern Baptist mission entities and the future budget of Johnson Ferry. Bryant and I spent six weeks copreaching a sermon series on the need to reach our neighbors and unreached people groups from around the world with the gospel of Jesus Christ. This would culminate with people bringing forward their offerings for what we hoped would be the largest single-day offering ever collected in the history of the church.

Sermon Series

Bryant: It was a joy to meet with Clay to talk through the sermon series we would do together. We planned for him to preach a three-week series by himself for the first three weeks after he arrived. Then, as we preached the series together, he would preach one week, and I would preach the next, and then in the later part of the transition, he would preach two Sundays, and I would preach one.

The second series we preached together focused on my final challenge to Johnson Ferry—to have the largest one-day offering in the history of the church for global missions. It would be called a "Great Commission Offering." Two-thirds of the offering would go to international and North American missions, and one-third of the offering would go to the ministry budget that is all about local and global ministries. A goal of $3 million dollars was set and shared with the church on that day.

Global missions and a passion for Christ's Great Commission have been the greatest "God thing" in the last twenty-five years of our history. We had always given generously to missions, but beginning in 1992 with a spring break mission trip with our high school students, people going on short-term trips around the globe had continued to grow. In the last five years (before Covid), about two thousand teenagers and adults were going on short-term mission trips each year. Out of this, we had sent out more than 140 units (families and individuals) into full-time vocational ministry. God worked powerfully in the lives of our people through giving, sending, and going in global missions. This offering would build on that legacy. And most of all, this offering would build the kingdom of God when the good news of Jesus was preached around the world. As I challenged the congregation to meet our goal on this offering, I asked them to do this in place of giving a love offering to Anne and me. This would be a much more meaningful offering. That seemed to get the attention of our church. People began to pray about what they would give. Even the children and student ministries set specific goals for the children and students to give. It also would be an opportunity to jump-start a new era of pastoral leadership with Clay. With Clay and me presenting the series together and leading the church together to rise to the challenge, it could be an exciting win for Christ's kingdom at the beginning of our new pastor's ministry.

Because so many at Johnson Ferry give online, we began the one-day offering on the Monday before that Sunday. This way the online givers could be sure to participate. And because so many of our people in a special offering give out of stock assets versus cash, we knew it would take most of the next week to process all the stock gifts and then know the final amount given. The anticipation was high. People came ready to give on that special Sunday, and the number who came forward to give was an inspiring sight.

On the Monday after the one-day offering on Sunday, the business office told us that they still had a long way to go in counting, but we had already surpassed the goal. By Friday evening of that week, the offering totaled more than $5.1 million—more than two million more than the goal. The end result was more than $5.5 million, all for missions. Praise the Lord!

You can imagine the excitement that Sunday as Clay and I shared what the congregation had given to the Great Commission. It was like God was saying, "I have blessed you all these years with your focus on the Great Commission, and I am going to keep blessing you in a greater way in the future." What a day of celebration and joy for Johnson Ferry to the glory of God for what He had done through His people.

Clay: What began as an idea turned into a true "God moment" as the people of Johnson Ferry rallied to be a part of something bigger than themselves. We blew far past our $3 million goal and were able to collect $5.5 million—all for the cause of the Great Commission. Not only would this money help get the gospel to the nations, but it would also provide a safety net for the church as we went through a time of transition. I can't think of a better way to start a ministry than with something as powerful as this.

If you had asked me going into this transition what would serve me best, I would have said that I wanted to take the primary leadership role from day one. After all, if God had called me to be the pastor, I wanted to be the pastor. I'm so glad we did something different. This four-month overlap was invaluable to me and to the church. I saw it as a stewardship. God was holding me accountable for two main goals during that time. The first was to honor Bryant as my predecessor, both publicly and privately. I prayed for him regularly and asked God to keep my ego in check, especially in the moments when I wanted to do otherwise. The second goal was to help him finish well. This can look different based on the gifts of the predecessor, but for us it meant colaboring with Bryant and doing all I could to help him run through the finish line of ministry at Johnson Ferry with as much tailwind as possible. I would remind myself of these two goals weekly, and doing so gave me a focus for how to approach the complexities of the transition. This also helped serve the church as they saw us work well together. I believe it helped dampen any anxiety they might have felt about the health and vitality of the church going forward. This transition was all a part of God's plan, and He was leading us all through this overlap.

The primary personal benefit of the overlap time I shared with Bryant was that we deepened a friendship and love for each other. Bryant's humility and intentionality were impressive to watch as he handled the "passing of the baton" with grace and dignity.

Bryant: Through this transition, people at Johnson Ferry kept asking me, "How are you doing?" "Are you doing okay?" "Are you enjoying retirement?" (I had to answer that one by reminding them I wasn't gone yet.) I think the congregation knew how much I love them. The overwhelming majority of my adult life was spent building and pastoring Johnson Ferry from the founding days meeting in an unleased doctor's office to where the church is today. It was a joy to tell them that Anne and I were doing fine. The peace we felt was supernatural because we love Johnson Ferry, and to let go of her after all these years was not easy. This inner peace was God's confirmation that we were obeying God's will to hand off the leadership role to a younger man.

At the same time, however, this peace came in many emotional moments. Realizing we were experiencing certain ministry events for the last time would fill me with tears. There was also great emotion when I felt overwhelmed with gratitude to God for how He had blessed our church. We were just filled with thanks to the Lord that He allowed us to have a part in all that He had done. The congregation knows I rarely shed tears, but in those last four months I shed more tears than I had in all of the thirty-seven previous years combined.

Chapter 12

THE HANDOFF

The final three-week series Clay and I preached together was titled "Transition." He preached the first sermon; then the next week I preached a sermon to Clay, and the congregation got to hear it. It focused on Paul's guidance to his successor Timothy who followed Paul as pastor of the church at Ephesus, a church that Paul had founded. The parallels to our situation of a young pastor following a founding pastor were obvious. It also allowed me to share some of the challenges and difficulties any pastor faces in a way that the congregation could better know how to pray for Clay.

Then on the final Sunday: (1) One of our elders shared with the congregation early in the service that the church was going to give Anne and me extended time away on sabbatical for six months.

This would give us a much needed break after thirty-eight years of ministry but also allow Clay to become the pastor. (2) Clay and I did the sermon together. I preached the first part. Then we had a symbolic handoff and prayer time for Clay. He closed out this sermon for that day.

I had heard and seen different ways that retiring senior pastors have conducted the handoff to their successors. The most common was "passing the baton." I used that as a sermon illustration versus doing it. Some pastors wash their successor's feet as a symbolic show of support to the new pastor. As I kept praying about how to do this, I thought back to how I had given my first three "preaching Bibles" to my three sons when I took them on a special trip to Normandy and we sat among those rows of white crosses on the beautiful lawn of that great cemetery. (About every five to seven years, I would wear out the Bible I was preaching from with notes and words and the margins and underlining and highlighting.) What could be more appropriate and more fitting for Johnson Ferry, for we are a church grounded in the Word for thirty-eight years. Giving Clay my most recent preaching Bible and challenging him to continue to preach the Word—to lead the church with the ultimate soul food (the Word of God) all the days of his ministry just seemed right. Then we called the elders—(six laymen and myself) to lay hands on Clay as he knelt before the Lord and the congregation asking God's blessing on his ministry.

One disadvantage we had at Johnson Ferry in moments like this is that it had to be repeated three times on Sunday morning with three consecutive hours of worship services. It was emotional handing that Bible to Clay in the first service. More emotional in the second service. Then when we came to that time in the third service, I was overcome with emotion: with the love I have for Johnson Ferry, with the love I have for preaching the Word, and with the gratitude that God had led us to His man to lead Johnson Ferry for years to come. It was a charge to Clay to faithfully feed the flock with God's life-transforming Word that is centered on Jesus and the gospel. The time had come. The handoff had occurred. After the elders had laid hands on Clay and prayed for him, Clay closed out this sermon that day. As he closed in prayer, Anne and I slipped out. It was important for the congregation to open their eyes and see one pastor, the man God had chosen. A new day had begun for Johnson Ferry!

Clay: On our last Sunday together, we preached a joint sermon. He preached the first half of the sermon from 2 Timothy 4, citing the apostle Paul's words of advice to a younger pastor, Timothy. At the end of his time, Bryant called the elders, Terrica, and me to the platform. He gave me his preaching Bible as a "son in the ministry." The elders then laid hands on me and commissioned me as their pastor. When they exited the platform, I finished the sermon, preaching the last few verses of the same text. It was a wonderful gesture about the continuity of the ministry and the endurance of God's Word.

I felt then, as I do now, that it is an honor not only to pastor Johnson Ferry but to follow Bryant Wright. We are not perfect men, but we serve a perfect Savior, Jesus Christ. Bryant's grace and leadership were guiding pillars throughout the search process, and all parties involved truly felt as though "God did this." I can't imagine the transition going any better than it did, and I know that the lessons I've learned in my early days at Johnson Ferry will serve me well many years from now when it's my time to leave.

EPILOGUE

People have asked—how did the transition go from one pastor to the next? The stats show that the successor who follows a long-tenured founding pastor has the lowest chance of success. My answer is, "Time will tell, but the transition couldn't have gone better."

I know this. My last six months at Johnson Ferry and the calling and serving together with Clay were some of the most meaningful and enjoyable days of pastoring Johnson Ferry in my thirty-eight-year tenure.

My role now is to support my successor—to pray for him regularly; to be available as he needs feedback, counsel, and encouragement; and to support him privately and publicly so that he is unhindered in following God's will in leading and pastoring Johnson Ferry. I look forward to the sequel of this story as God uses His man, Clay

Smith, to lead Christ's church at Johnson Ferry to stay focused on Jesus and carry out His Great Commission for years to come.